Practical
Karate

Self-Defense in
Special Situations

Practical
Karate 6

Self-Defense in Special Situations

M. Nakayama
Donn F. Draeger

Tuttle Publishing
Boston • Rutland, Vermont • Tokyo

Disclaimer
The adoption and application of the material offered in this book is at the reader's
discretion and sole responsibility. The Author and Publisher of this book are not
responsible in any manner whatsoever for any injury that may occur indirectly or
directly from the use of this book. Since the physical activities described herein may be
too strenuous in nature for some readers to engage in safely, please consult a physician
prior to training. The specific self-defense practices illustrated in this book may not be
justified in every particular situation or under applicable federal, state or local law.
Neither the Author or the Publisher make any warranty or representation regarding the
legality or appropriateness of any technique mentioned in this book.

Library of Congress Catalog Card Number: 98-87646
ISBN 0-8048-0486-9

DISTRIBUTED BY

NORTH AMERICA
Tuttle Publishing
RR 1 Box 231-5
North Clarendon, VT 05759
Tel: (802) 773-8930
Tel: (800) 526-2778

SOUTHEAST ASIA
Berkeley Books Pte. Ltd.
5 Little Road #08-01
Singapore 536983
Tel: (65) 280-3320
Fax: (65) 280-6290

JAPAN
Tuttle Shokai Ltd.
1-21-13, Seki
Tama-ku, Kawasaki-shi
Kanagawa-ken 214, Japan
Tel: (044) 833-0225
Fax: (044) 822-0413

First edition
07 06 05 04 03 02 01   00 99 98   10 9 8 7 6 5 4 3 2 1

Printed in Singapore

TABLE OF CONTENTS

Authors' Foreword 7

Preface 11

Essential Points 14

Chapter One: AUTOMOBILE SITUATIONS 15
Rear Seat Bare-handed Choke; Rear Seat Judo Arm Choke; Rear Seat Judo Lapel Choke; Rear Seat Garrotte; Rear Seat Double Assailant Threat; Single Assailant Outside Threat; Double Assailant Outside Threat

Chapter Two: TIED HAND SITUATIONS 55
Frontal Tie—Single Assailant, Single Punch; Frontal Tie—Single Assailant, Kicking Attack; Frontal Tie—Single Assailant, Kick and Double Punch Attack; Frontal Tie—Single Assailant, Hold and Punch Attack; Rear Tie—Single Assailant, Grasp and Punch; Rear Tie—Double Assailant, Rough-up

Chapter Three: SWITCHBLADE, CHAIN, MEATCLEAVER AND RAZOR ATTACKS 91
Frontal Free Threat—Switchblade; Frontal Free Threat—Chain; Frontal Free Threat—Meatcleaver; Frontal Free Threat—Razor

Chapter Four: HANDGUN ATTACKS 113
Frontal Free Threat; Frontal Search; Rear Free Threat

AUTHORS' FOREWORD

THERE is perhaps no greater disservice to man than the creation of false confidence in his ability to defend himself. Whether this false confidence is manifested in his nation's armed might, or his own personal ability, the result is the same, though of different proportions, when tested—*disaster!*

The current *karate* boom in the U.S.A. has instilled in many would-be experts a serious, false sense of security. This is the natural outgrowth of a human psychological weakness. Everyone wishes to be physically fit and able to defend himself and his loved ones from danger and quickly turns to any sure-fire guarantee of such abilities.

Unscrupulous and unqualified self-appointed *karate* "experts" daily exploit this human weakness and prey on an innocent, unsuspecting public. This grossly perpetrated fraud is based on the quick learning of ancient mysterious Oriental combative forms such as *karate*, and almost always makes its appeal colorful through the use of adjectives such as "super," "destructive," "terror tactics," and guarantees you mastery of an art that will make you "fear no man." All such get-skillful-quickly schemes should be carefully investigated before taking them seriously, for true *karate* involves constant dedication to training and is never a short-course method. Choose your instructor carefully.

On the other hand, authentic teachers of *karate* do exist in the U.S.A., and their teachings have full merit. These teachings are deeply rooted in traditional, classical *karate* and require a liberal application of patience and regular training to develop expert *karate* skill. There are various schools that stem from historic Oriental antiquity, all of which are legitimate and have both merits and shortcomings. The choice of

7

which school to follow can be decided upon only by the interested party.

The average person is confined to a daily life that requires of him a heavy investment in time and energy in order to earn a living. Leisure time is generally at a minimum and it is spent at less enervating pursuits than classical *karate* practice, a demanding and rigorous "pastime." But the need for a practical system of self-defense designed for the average person is more evident than ever before. Police files give mute testimony to the increasing number of robberies, assaults, and other vicious crimes.

In self-defense situations involving assailants armed with extremely dangerous weapons or those situations which are unusual due to circumstances of one's physical location or because of the nature of the method the assailant or assailants are using, each situation involves and carries with it a degree of danger beyond normal attack circumstances. Accordingly, *karate* techniques must be learned thoroughly and executed as automatic responses to any series of happenings if serious injury or death is to be avoided.

Like its predecessors—Books One, Two, Three, and Four—this book is a categorized collection of self-defense situations and recommended *karate* responses. It is written for every male person and brings to him a chance to improve his personal self-defense abilities without engaging in the severe discipline and dedication to daily training required by classical *karate*. It is not an exhaustive survey of *karate* methods, but it contains methods that give direct consideration to easy learning for the average person. All methods described in this book are workable *karate* self-defense responses based on meeting single and multiple assailants. The responses are simplified, direct methods of self-defense. If you have already studied and practiced the necessary *karate* fundamentals found in Book One of this series, the situations in this volume will be easier to learn. Otherwise, after reading about the situations and responses herein you may find it necessary to turn to Book One, the fundamentals book, and find the necessary movements and practice exercises that are required to make these responses work effectively.

On the other hand, authentic teachers of *karate* do exist in the U.S.A., and their teachings have full merit. These teachings are deeply rooted in traditional, classical *karate* and require a liberal application of patience and regular training to develop expert *karate* skill. There are various schools that stem from historic Oriental antiquity, all of which mere reading and one or two rehearsals of each response in this book will not produce effectiveness.

The authors are indebted to the Japan Karate Association for the use of their facilities and hereby acknowledge with pleasure the assistance of those members and officials who have made this book possible. Additional thanks are due to Y. Jinguji, whose excellent photographic skills have contributed greatly toward the easy readability of this book ; to William A. Fuller, Paul Nutio, Dave Jinks, and Charles Gauch, who posed as "assailants," and to Mr. and Mrs. Frank P. Kreiger, Jr. of Tokyo whose private facilities served as background for many of the situations.

Tokyo, Japan

M. NAKAYAMA

DONN F. DRAEGER

PREFACE

KARATE is a martial art developed by people who were prohibited the use of weapons, thus making it a *defensive* art. When one is attacked, the empty hands (which the word *karate* implies) are quite sufficient to defend oneself if one is highly skilled in the art. However, to become highly skilled takes exacting discipline, both mental and physical. The main purpose of this series of six books is to avoid the advanced techniques of *karate* which require many years of study and instead to describe simplified *karate* technique as easy-to-learn responses to typical self-defense situations.

Karate is highly esteemed as a sport, self-defense, and as a physical attribute for athletics in general. It is becoming increasingly popular in schools, offices, factories, law enforcement agencies and the armed services, varying in degree as required by the respective wants and needs.

In response to the many requets for treatment of *karate* purely as a defensive system, it is hoped that the information contained in this series of six books will be more than sufficient to meet these requests. In conclusion, if readers of this series of books will fully understand the principles and ideals of *karate,* taking care to use its techniques with discretion, they will reflect great credit to this magnificent art.

ZENTARO KOSAKA
Former Foreign Minister
of Japan
Director, Japan Karate Association

11

THE FIRST and most complete and authoritative text on *karate* in the English language, titled *Karate: The Art of "Empty Hand" Fighting,* by Hidetaka Nishiyama and Richard C. Brown, instructor and member of the Japan Karate Association respectively, made its appearance in 1960. It presents *karate* in its three main aspects—a healthful physical art, an exciting sport, and an effective form of self-defense. As such, it is considered the standard textbook of the Japan Karate Association and adequately serves both as a reference and instructional manual for novice and expert alike.

Many students of *karate* find the study of classical *karate* somewhat impractical in modern Western society, chiefly because time limitations prohibit sufficient practice. These students generally desire to limit their interpretations of *karate* to self-defense aspects. With this sole training objective in mind, a series of six books is being prepared which describes in simplified form the necessary *karate* movements for personal defense that can be learned by anybody of average physical abilities.

The authors, Mr. Nakayama, Chief Instructor of the Japan Karate Association and Donn F. Draeger, a well-known instructor of combative arts, bring a balanced, practical, and functional approach to *karate,* based on the needs of Western society. As a specialized series of *karate* texts, these are authentic books giving full and minute explanations of the practical art of self-defense. All movements are performed in normal daily dress and bring the performer closer to reality.

Today, *karate* is attracting the attention of the whole world and is being popularized at an amazing rate. I sincerely hope that this series of books will be widely read as a useful reference for the lovers of *karate* all over the world. It is further hoped that the techniques shown in this series of books need never be used by any reader, but should an emergency arise making their use unavoidable, discretion in application should be the keynote.

M. Takagi

MASATOMO TAKAGI
Standing Director and
Head of the General Affairs
Department of the Japan
Karate Association

12

Practical
Karate

*Self-Defense in
Special Situations*

ESSENTIAL POINTS

1. Never underestimate your assailant. Always assume he is dangerous.

2. Stepping, weight shifting, and body turning are the keys to avoiding an assailant's attack and bringing him into position for your counterattack.

3. Turn your body as a unit, not in isolated parts, for maximum effect.

4. If the ground is rough, bumpy, or slick, you may be unable to maneuver as you would like. Simple weight shifting and twisting of your hips may be all that is possible. Don't get too fancy in your footwork.

5. Your body can only act efficiently in *karate* techniques if you make it a stable foundation, working from braced feet and a balanced position as you deliver your blow.

6. Coordinate your blocking or striking action to the assailant's target area with your stepping, weight shifting, and body turning, for maximum effect.

7. Do not oppose superior power with power, but seek to harmonize it with your body action and direct it to your advantage.

8. Seek to deliver your striking actions to the assailant's anatomical weak points (vital points) rather than to hard, resistant areas.

9. After delivering the striking action to your assailant's target area, you must never lose sight of him and you should be constantly alert for a continuation of his attack.

10. Use discretion in dealing out punishment to any assailant. Fit the degree of punishment to the situation.

Chapter One
AUTOMOBILE SITUATIONS

THERE is no law or formula, natural or man-made, that requires an assailant or assailants to attack their intended victim in a predetermined pattern and/or with standard design tactics and weapons. Both premeditated and spontaneous attacks often feature unusual places, tactics, and/or weapons. Their form is limitless, subject only to the expressions of the psychologically-disturbed mind making these attacks.

Being attacked by an assailant or assailants while in an automobile must receive careful attention and consideration as a delicate situation, even more difficult to defend against than when outside and free to move around. Much of what is done borrows liberally from commoner situations described in Books Two, Three, and Four, and requires that you take the proper defensive response if you wish to avoid serious injury or even death. Here too, in situations involving an automobile, mistakes may be costly.

The person highly trained in *karate* techniques is able to meet such unusual situations with confidence, but *not without difficulty*. What follows in this chapter are responses appropriate to the hypothetical situations described; you, as an average person, will find these responses within your capabilities. The responses cover the minimum necessary principles with which to effectively meet the unusual attacks by single and multiple assailants.

All responses described in this chapter must be practiced with partners. Begin slowly, so that you have complete knowledge of what you are trying to do. Gradually speed up the attack sttuations and your responses in meeting them. Seek to build an automatic response by frequent practices several times a week.

Practice in normal daily garb and do not limit yourself to smooth, flat surfaces such as an ordinary street after leaving the automobile. Try to get some practice on grass, gravel, and unpaved surfaces—all of which will bring you closer to the actual conditions with which you will likely be faced in these emergencies.

The responses in this chapter are given in terms of one side, right or left, but in many instances, the other side may be practiced, by simply applying corresponding instructions. You will note that the automobile used is a right-hand drive model.

While your first response may satisfy the situation by neutralizing or knocking out the assailant, never relax your guard after making a response. Be prepared to continue your action with a continued alertness over the assailant(s). If you fail to do this you may become another statistic in the already large list of daily fatalities caused by attackers working as shown in this chapter.

REAR SEAT BARE-HANDED CHOKE

Situation: An assailant is choking you with his bare hands around your neck from the back seat of your automobile as you sit parked, at the wheel. He has risen from his seat. Your movement is highly restricted.

Response: At his grasp, tense your neck muscles, brace both your feet on the floor of the car. Twist slightly in your seat to your left. Make a tight fist with your left hand and raise that arm so that you can pass your left arm, elbow first, over the back of the car seat. Picture.

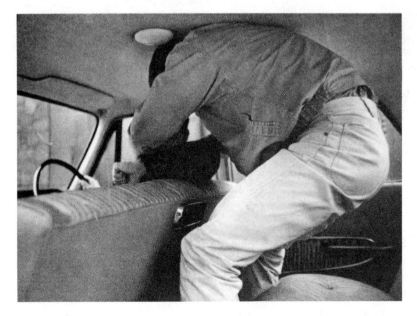

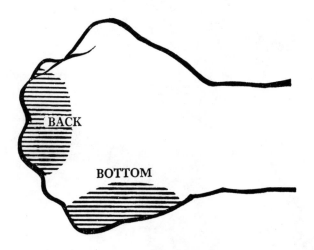

BACK

BOTTOM

As your left arm comes over the car seat, twist hard to your left and strike the assailant hard in his left rib area or mid-section using your Bottom Fist directly into either of those targets. Sketch. This final action can be seen on the next page.

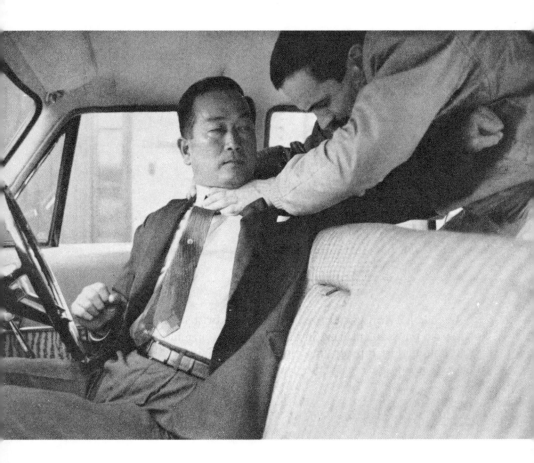

Keypoints: Do not try to strike without first passing your striking arm over the back of the car seat.

REAR SEAT JUDO ARM CHOKE

Situation: An assailant is choking you from the back seat of your automobile as you sit parked, at the wheel. He has not risen in his seat, but has merely leaned forward to encircle your neck with his right arm and is trying to mug you with his idea of the so-called Judo "naked" choke. He increases the choking power by pulling his right hand with his left. Your movement is highly restricted.

Response: Tense your neck muscles and brace both feet on the floor of the car. Twist slightly to your left and immediately pull his left hand/arm downward by the action of your left hand placed on top of his left wrist. Begin raising your right arm, forming that hand as a Hand Spear. Picture.

22

Increase the downward pull of your left hand as you twist hard to your left, turning your head away from his right elbow. Drive your Hand Spear into his facial region, if necessary, making repeated hard attacks aimed at his eyes. This action can be seen on the next page.

Keypoints: Struggling to break the choke is generally useless. Execute your response immediately upon feeling the choke being placed. Your left hand downward pulling action must precede your Hand Spear attack.

24

REAR SEAT JUDO LAPEL CHOKE

Situation: An assailant, working from the rear seat of your automobile, is attempting to place a Judo "sliding lapel" choke on you, using the lapels of your jacket. He has come up close behind you as you sit at the wheel of your parked car. Your movement is highly restricted.

25

Response: At his grasping of your lapels, tense your neck muscles and brace both feet on the floor of the car; grip the steering wheel firmly with your right hand. Twist slightly left in your seat as you brace against the steering wheel, and raise your left arm, elbow held high and that hand formed as a tight fist, thumb down. Picture.

26

Continue your bracing actions and twist more to your left as you deliver an Elbow Sideward Strike, using your left arm, hard into his facial area. This action can be seen on the next page.

Keypoints: It is essential that you do nothing to interfere with his gripping of your lapels; with his hands occupied, your response has a better target and thus a better chance for success which might otherwise be blocked if he detaches one or both hands.

28

REAR SEAT GARROTTE

Situation: As you sit at the wheel of your automobile, parked, an assailant attacks you with a rope garrotte action from the rear seat. He has slipped the rope around your neck and is choking you with a cross-handed action. Your movement is highly restricted.

Response 1: As you feel the rope settle around your neck, tense your neck muscles and drive backward in your seat, going with the force of the rope as much as possible. Brace your feet on the floor of the car, and grip the steering wheel with your right hand. Raise your free left arm, hand held as a tight fist with an extended knuckle (see sketch). Arch back in your seat, twisting a bit to your left as you reach up over the back of the seat and drive your fist into the assailant's facial/side head region. Picture. This final action can be seen on page 32.

Response 2: As the rope settles around your neck, brace your feet hard against the car floor, tense your neck muscles, and twist hard to your left. Raise both arms, placing the left arm on the back of the seat as you form a Hand Spear with your right hand. Turn to face the assailant as much as you can as you arch back in your seat. Drive the Hand Spear hard into his facial area, aiming at his eyes. Picture. This final action may be seen on the next page.

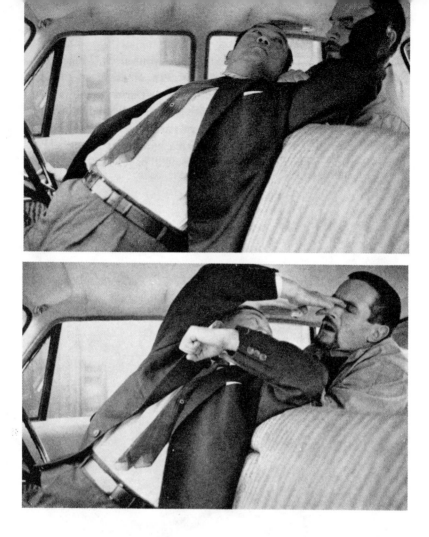

Keypoints: Response 1. You must drive back hard in your seat to get close to the target.

Response 2. A fuller twist is needed than in Response 1. Your left arm must clear the back of the seat prior to using your Hand Spear.

REAR SEAT DOUBLE ASSAILANT THREAT

Situation: You are in the rear seat of an automobile, sandwiched between two assailants. A " being-taken-for-a-ride " atmosphere prevails. Your movement is highly restricted.

Response 1: Keep your feet braced on the floor of the car, but do not tense your body to warn your assailants. Go into action when they are restraining you very loosely, by using a double Elbow Sideward Strike of each elbow (strike twice with each) hard into their facial regions, coming a bit forward in the seat as you strike. Picture, top.

Response 2: If your assailants are restraining you somewhat less than loosely, keep your feet braced and deliver an Elbow Sideward Strike to the assailant who is restraining you least (left-hand assailant shown), striking with your elbow hard into his facial region. Lean forward a bit in your seat and twist into him as much as you can as you drive your elbow into the target. Picture, bottom. Immediately anticipate

the assailant on the other side by placing a Sweeping Block against his reaching right arm, using your left hand on the inside of his forearm just below his elbow. Pull that arm forward as you twist to your right to deliver an Elbow Sideward Strike with your right arm, hard into his facial region. This final action can be seen on the next page.

Keypoints: Response 1. This action depends upon surprise. It may not be final and you must be prepared to go to other defenses.

Response 2. Your Sweeping Block must be powerfully made to be effective. Use it even if the assailant is just sitting there.

SINGLE ASSAILANT OUTSIDE THREAT

Situation: You are seated at the wheel of your car, and are parked. An assailant, standing outside of the car is threatening to do you bodily harm; he is apparently unarmed. He has reached for and is opening the door; there is no time to lock the door.

Response 1: At the time he opens the car door, grip the steering wheel of your car firmly with both hands and brace your left foot firmly on the floor of the car.

As the door swings open and the assailant steps near to scuffle with you, raise your right foot slightly from the floor, cocking your ankle by turning the sole of the shoe slightly inward. Picture.

Before the assailant can lay his hands upon you, go into action by leaning slightly away from him as you brace your left foot firmly on

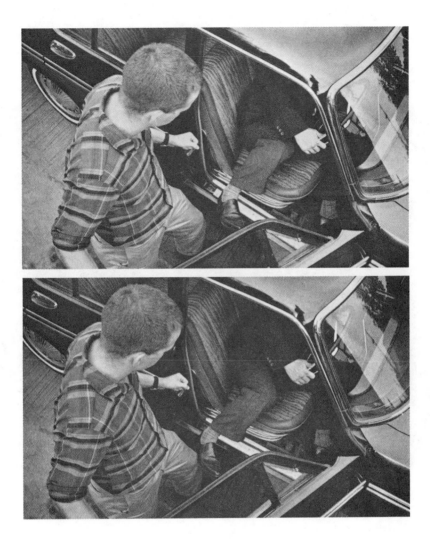

the floor. Drive a Foot Edge kick action hard into his advanced (left shown) leg at a point just at the knee, by using your right leg; brace firmly with your left foot and hands on the steering wheel. Pictures, above. The final action can be seen on the next page.

Keypoints: You must steady your body with your left foot on the floor and your grips on the steering wheel prior to the assailant opening the door. Time your kick as he opens the door and steps forward.

40

Response 2: As your assailant opens the door he steps close to you and grabs you by a lapel or by your tie with his left hand before you can execute Response One. He is preparing to jerk you out of the car and hammer you with his cocked right hand.

At his grasp and pull, go into action by swinging your right hand from across your body, hand formed as a Knife-hand or as a tight fist; your palm facing you. Deliver either a Knife-hand into his midsection or a Back Fist into his groin region by whipping your right arm toward him as you turn slightly to face him, twisting in your seat. Pictures. The final actions can be seen on the next page.

Keypoints: It is essential to harmonize with your assailant's pulling actions. If he overpowers the pull, you may have to step one or both feet onto the ground outside of the car to stabilize yourself prior to delivering an effective blow.

Response 3: If, after opening the car door, the assailant closes in on you by stepping forward with his right leg and reaches for you with his right hand, grabbing your lapel or tie (see picture), harmonize with his pull and slide out of the seat toward him, placing one or both feet on the ground. Remain seated.

Do not seek to remove his right hand grasp, rather encourage it to remain tightly gripping your garments; it will offer an excellent target against which to operate. Face into your assailant as you sit, bracing your foot (or feet) on the ground and simultaneously execute a combined Forearm Block and Palm-heel Block directly against the elbow of his right arm. Pictures above.

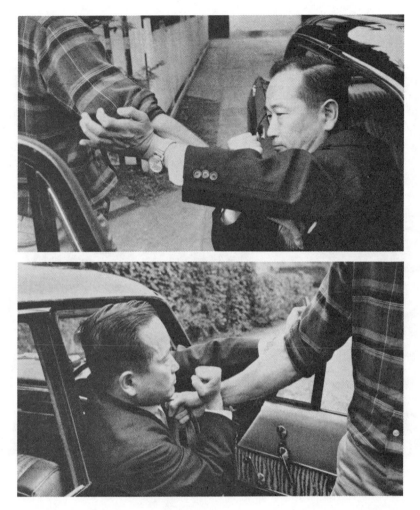

Deliver the Forearm Block with your right arm, hand held as a tight fist, knuckles away from you, so that you bring the hard outer edge of your forearm forcefully into the soft inner side-edge of the assailant's right forearm. Deliver the Palm-heel block with your left arm, hand brought forcefully against the assailant's outer right arm in a sideways fashion, contacting the assailant's arm just above his elbow joint. Pictures above. The final action can be seen on the next page.

Keypoints: It is essential that you be alert for punching actions of the assailant's left hand. Be sure to brace your body, with feet on the ground, and to harmonize with his pull. The combined actions of the Forearm Block and Palm-heel Block must be simultaneously delivered.

DOUBLE ASSAILANT OUTSIDE THREAT

Situation: Two assailants are menacing you from outside of your car as you sit parked, behind the wheel. The assailant seeking to open the car door is armed with a club-like instrument; the other, stands alongside the front fender on the driver's side and appears to be unarmed.

Response: As the assailant opens the door, go into action before he can do more than close in on you. Deliver a backward kicking action using the heel of your left leg, hard into the groin region of that assailant. See picture above. This is done as follows:

48

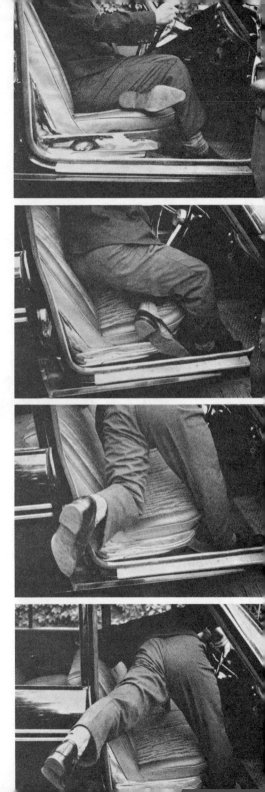

Prior to the assailant opening the car door, you must position yourself with your left leg tucked under your body. Your right foot is placed on the floor of the car and is used as a brace and a pivot point on which to turn your body. Your right hand, grips the steering wheel firmly and gives additional support to your body while your left hand may be placed on the front seat of the car, or along its back upper edge (shown) for the same reasons. See series of pictures. The kick action requires you to turn your body, using your right foot as the support-pivot with knee slightly bent, and to face downward into the seat.

The kick may not knock the assailant out, but only drive him backward. This will at least give you time to step out of the car (backing), using the extended kicking left leg to step directly to the ground after kicking; push with both hands to speed your exit. Pivot immediately on your left foot, turning your body to the right to step

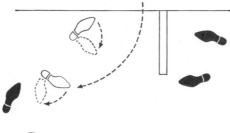

and face into the club-bearing assailant; as you turn, push the car door fully open to "screen" yourself from the other assailant who may be closing in on you. See pictures on these two pages and the diagrams. As the club-bearing assailant charges forward, avoid his overhead club attack by bringing your right arm across your body

and upward, hand formed as a Knife-hand, to deliver a hard blow against his club arm underside, near his wrist; twist your hips to the right as you deliver the blocking action and hold your left arm, hand held in a tight fist, knuckles downward, at your left hip. See pictures this page. If your club-bearing assailant is knocked out or is not charging you this manuever will not be wasted for it will keep him at bay and you may move directly from this point against the other assailant.

After blocking the club-bearing assailant's club arm, twist your hips hard to your right, as you grip the assailant's club arm at the wrist with your right hand, and execute a single-handed downward Grasping Block to pull the assailant forward and off balance. Simultaneously deliver either a Forefist hard into his mid-section or groin region using your left hand, or an Elbow Forward Strike (shown) with your left arm hard into the same target areas; the choice is largely dependent upon the distance between you and your assailant. If he is close, the elbow will be effective, if he is farther away, it must be the Forefist. See picture. Turn immediately after this blow to face the other assailant by pivoting to your left as shown in the diagram below. The final facing action and defensive posture can be seen on the next page.

Keypoints: In the car, you must fold your left leg prior to the assailant getting the car door open. Use the action of your left foot kick to step to the ground after the blow lands. Turn to face club-bearing assailant expecting the club attack; the Knife-hand blocking action can be varied to block at different heights and will work against a lower club swing as well.

Chapter Two
TIED HAND SITUATIONS

DEFENDING yourself when you have full use of your hands is no simple matter, but when your hands have been bound, you will suffer the loss of much effective *karate* defense. Yet, there are some actions that may aid you.

Hands which have been tied in front, permit effective blocking, deflecting, and striking actions which must rely upon correctly executed footwork and body twisting mechanics to be forceful enough to defend the person so restrained. Hands tied in the rear offer little or no aid in roles of blocking, deflecting, and striking actions, and are primarily useful only in aiding balance for the only avenue of defensive response left to such a restrained victim—that of kicking actions.

The person highly trained in *karate* techniques is able to meet such delicate situations with confidence, but *not without difficulty*. What follows in this chapter are responses appropriate to the hypothetical situations described; they will be found to be a bit difficult for all but the most agile of average citizens, but there is no other course of action than to train in these responses if one is to avoid the serious consequences of the emergencies that provoke them.

All responses described in this chapter must be practiced with a training partner(s). Begin slowly, so that you have complete knowledge of what you are trying to achieve. Gradually speed up the attack situations and your responses in meeting them. Seek to build an automatic response habit by frequent practices, several times per week.

Practice in normal daily dress and do not limit yourself to smooth, flat surfaces such as a gym floor. Try to get some practice on grass, gravel, and unpaved surfaces, all of which will bring realism into the situations such as you may be called on to face when confronted with similar real-life attacks.

The responses are given in terms of one side, right or left, but in many instances, by simply using corresponding instructions, you can make the response from the other side.

Your first response may satisfy the situation by neutralizing or knocking out the assailant(s), but it is essential that you never relax your vigil after making that response. You must be prepared to continue your defense. If you fail to heed this advice, you can easily become the victim of a more enraged and extremely dangerous assailant(s).

FRONTAL TIE-SINGLE ASSAILANT, SINGLE PUNCH

Situation: Your hands have been tied in front of you. An assailant, facing you, is about to strike you with his right fist. There is sufficient room in which to move about.

Response 1: As the assailant swings a straight right-handed punch at your face, step backward a short distance with your right foot and simultaneously execute an X-Block with your tied hands in front of your head. See diagram and picture. Catch the assailant's right arm near the wrist with your your right hand and perform a one-handed Grasping Block action with the hand by pulling the assailant's punching arm downward and forward sharply; simultaneously deliver a front snap kick with the ball of your right foot, hard into his groin region (see pictures above, bottom of these two pages). The final action may be seen on page 60.

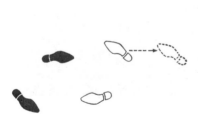

Response 2: If the assailant swings a round-house right at your head, you have a bit more time in which to move, and you may choose to leave out the X-Block. Lower your body by bending your knees and duck low under the assailant's swing. Drive a double-arm Forefist punch hard into his mid-section or groin, by lunging a bit forward and using both hands, formed as tight fists. See two pictures above. The final action can be seen on the next page.

Keypoints: Response 1: Do not step back before the assailant punches. Time your step with his punch; block with the step. The X-Block is made straight up in front of you. Your Grasping Block action must pull the assailant forward into your kick.

Response 2: It may be necessary to step in closer to the assailant in order to make your double-handed Forefist striking action. Duck low and lunge forward to protect against any back-hand action the assailant may use after missing his original round-house.

60

Response 3: At the assailant's right-hand straight jab, step backward with your left foot, turning the toes outward and simultaneously execute the X-Block with both hands up underneath his punching arm. See top picture and diagram.

Keeping the X-Block in contact with his attacking arm as much as you can, step quickly in toward him with your right foot to a position just inside of his advanced left foot; lower your body a bit by bending your knees and begin to detach your X-Block. See middle picture and diagram. Drive a hard Elbow Sideward Strike, using your right arm, simultaneously with your stepping action, into his midsection or rib area as you lunge forward; stay under his punching arm. See bottom picture. The final action can be seen on the next page.

Keypoints: Deliver the striking action, as you step forward to reinforce its effect.

62

FRONTAL TIE-SINGLE ASSAILANT, KICKING ATTACK

Situation: Your hands are tied in front of you and an assailant is preparing to attack you from in front; he has tried to kick you, but but has just missed. You have plenty of room in which to move around.

63

Response: Anticipate another kick, coming from his rearmost foot. At the kick, avoid it by quickly turning your body; draw your left leg around behind you in a short arc to a position that allows his kick to miss you. See above picture and diagram on the next page.

Bring your tied hands near your groin region, and if necessary used them in a downward X-Block fashion to stop the kick, dropping your hips a bit to give force to the block (not shown).

Deliver an Elbow Forward Strike hard into his mid-section by stepping forward with your right foot, toes turned inward toward him to position just outside of his left support foot (see diagram and picture next page). Lunge forward as you strike. The final action can be seen on page 66.

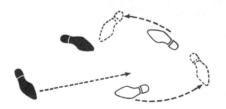

Keypoints: You must keep your upper body upright as you turn (block) and deliver your striking action.

66

FRONTAL TIE-SINGLE ASSAILANT, KICK
AND DOUBLE PUNCH ATTACK

Situation: Your hands have been tied in front of you. An assailant is facing you and has faked a double hand action upward to distract you from the kick he is about to deliver with his rearmost foot.

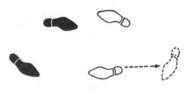

Response : At the kick, step backward with your left foot, turning those toes outward; simultaneously lower your hips and drive a downward X-Block hard against the shin of his kicking leg. Diagram, top and middle picture.

His kick blocked, the assailant returns his kicking leg to the ground and immediately swings a left hook at your head. Meet that attack by driving an X-Block upward under his attacking arm, contacting it near his wrist. Previous page, bottom left picture. Blocked again, the assailant continues his attack by an uppercut action of his right hand; detach your upper position X-Block to meet this new threat as you drive that X-Block downward. Previous page, bottom right picture.

Block his uppercut with an X-Block hard against his right forearm near the wrist. Bottom left-hand picture. Immediately after blocking, step your right foot foward a bit to a position outside of and a bit to the rear of his lead left foot, simultaneously delivering a hard Elbow Forward Strike with your right arm into his mid-section or groin region. Diagram and bottom right-hand picture. The final action can be seen on the next page.

Keypoints: A sense of timing is essential to avoid premature blocking actions and detachments from blocking.

FRONTAL TIE-SINGLE ASSAILANT, HOLD AND PUNCH ATTACK

Situation: A frontal assailant is holding your right arm; both your hands have been tied together and positioned in front of you. The assailant is preparing to punch you with his right hand. There is sufficient room to move.

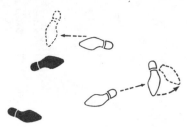

Response: Before your assailant can punch, go into action by simultaneously stepping forward with your right foot, toes turned in toward the assailant, to a position just outside of his advanced left foot, and twisting hard to your left to jam your right elbow forward in the direction of your twist. Diagram and top pictures. This action brings strong leverage against the assailant's grasp. Bottom picture.

Quickly step away from your assailant, taking a short step to your left with your left foot, turning that foot so the toes point in the direction of your movement (diagram preceeding page). Shift your weight to your left leg, keeping that knee slightly bent and draw up your right leg. Lean slightly away from your assailant and deliver a Foot Edge kick hard into any available target such as the assailant's advanced left knee (shown) or his groin region (diagram). This final action may be seen (mid-section and knee) on the next page.

Keypoints: When you twist to your left, keep one point pressure as a pivotal point for your right arm, that is, his grasp; do not tug to release your arm. Do not use arm power alone, twist your hips. The knee is a more suitable target for the average man.

REAR TIE-SINGLE ASSAILANT, GRASP AND PUNCH

Situation: Your hands have been tied behind your back. A frontal assailant is gripping your neck or lapel with his left hand and is preparing to strike you in the face with his right hand. There is room in which to move.

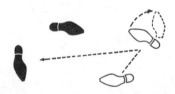

Response 1: You have been caught in a left front-facing posture. Pivot quickly on your right foot, turning the toes of that foot to your right (diagram), then quickly shift your weight to your right leg and deliver a Foot Edge hard into your assailant's right knee joint. Top picture. Immediately after kicking, bring your kicking leg down, positioning that foot behind you and close to your weighted right foot, taking care to turn the toes of your left foot so that they point into the assailant. Top two pictures, next page.

76

Continue your action by shifting your weight over this newly-placed left leg, keeping that knee bent slightly. Deliver a Ball of the Foot kick in a semi-circular arc fashion with your right leg, hard into his rib area as you twist your hips forcefully to your left and pivot on the weighted left foot. Bottom two pictures, this page. The final action can be seen on the next page.

Keypoints: Do not struggle against his left-hand hold. Twist your hips to the left after stepping back with your left foot and drop your hips a bit as you deliver the second kick.

78

Response 2: You are caught in a right front-facing posture and cannot work the first response effectively. Do not struggle against his left-hand grip, but go into action before he can strike you.

Twist your body hard to your left, shifting your weight to your left leg but keeping your feet in place; bring your shoulder hard against his gripping arm. Picture.

Continuing twisting to your left and his grip may loosen or become detached (shown), but regardless, quickly reverse your twist action by turning hard to your right, using your right foot as a pivot and simultaneously face into your assailant. Bring your left foot off the ground and deliver a Front Knee kick hard into his groin region. Pictures, next page. The final action can be seen on page 82.

Keypoints: This double twisting action must be powerfully done and without delay.

82

Response 3: If after making the first twist (left) away from your assailant in Response 2, you find yourself too far from the assailant to turn back into him and knee him, or if he is pushing you so hard that the second twist is impossible, you must take some other action.

Shift your weight to your left leg, bending that knee slightly as you simultaneously draw up your right leg, thigh parallel to the

ground (picture above). Deliver a Foot Edge, using your right foot, hard into his groin or mid-section (shown). Picture next page. If this maneuver is too difficult or for some other reason impractical, or should continuation of your kicking action be required, drive your right Foot Edge hard into his advanced leg knee (left shown) or stamp your heel into his advanced left foot instep. Both these additional actions can be seen on page 86.

Keypoints: Your weighted left leg must keep a slightly bent knee position to aid your balance. Be alert to continue your kicking attacks.

86

REAR TIE-DOUBLE ASSAILANT, ROUGH UP

Situation: Two assailants, one on each side of you, intend to rough you up. Your hands have been tied behind you. There is plenty of space to move in. The assailant on your right is gripping you and pulling you forward; the other is menacing you and intends to strike you.

Response: At the right-hand assailant's pull, do not struggle, but blend with his actions. Pivot quickly on your right foot, turning your toes to point directly into him. Swing your left leg forward to snap kick the frontal assailant in the groin with the ball of your left foot, or using a Front Knee Kick, knee him similarly (shown). Diagram and picture.

Without hesitation, anticipate the rear assailant who may be closing in on you, by stepping your left kicking leg to the ground immediately after the kick (kneeing), positioning that foot just inside of the assailant's right foot (diagram). Deliver a Rear Kick using your right heel hard into the rear assailant's groin or mid-section by shifting your weight to your newly-placed left leg, bending that knee slightly and thrusting backward with your right leg. Diagram and top pictures next page. This final action can be seen on page 90.

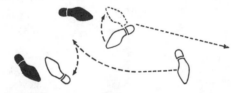

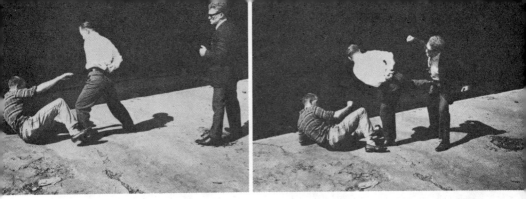

You may elect, after kicking (kneeing) the frontal assail ant, to pivot to your left to face your rear assailant. Do this by swinging your kicking/kneeing left leg directly backward in an arc, positioning that foot as shown in the diagram; twist your hips hard to your left to aid the turning and pivot on your weight right foot. Diagram. Shift your body weight to your left leg and deliver a front snap kick using the ball of your right foot, hard into the assailant's groin or mid-section (shown). Pictures below and diagram. The final action can be seen on the next page.

Keypoints: Do not resist the first assailant's pull action. Pivotal action and a sense of timing are critical. Study them thoroughly.

Chapter Three
SWITCHBLADE, CHAIN, MEATCLEAVER, AND RAZOR ATTACKS

ALL ATTACKS made with the switchblade, the chain, the meatcleaver, and the razor, are extremely dangerous emergencies.

The assailant wielding any of these instruments must be treated with extreme caution and it is highly imperative that your responses be the right ones and accurately placed if you are to survive. Multiple assailants armed with these weapons, confronting a single defender, are an almost impossible situation for the average man. *Karate* experts, highly trained, can meet these situations with confidence, but not without *extreme* difficulty. Yet, you as the less-than-expert, must have some knowledge of what to do when faced with these dangers.

The switchblade knife when open is to be treated as an ordinary knife in situations shown in Book Four. It is however, the object of this text to deal with it at the moment of its opening, a time when it has an inherent weakness that makes instantaneously executed responses effective.

The chain is a vicious weapon which can whip a victim into a bloody pulp or leave him a mass of broken bones and skin. Defenders must do one of two things to make effective defenses against it. First, you must stay *outside* of its swing radius, avoiding its blows completely until escape or a "jump in contact" can be made with the assailant out of position. Second, you can get *inside* of its swing radius, where the chain can do no great damage to you; there you can deal with the assailant as you would an ordinary attacker in Books Two and Three. If you are forced to collide with the swing radius of the attacker's chain, you must choose some target which is relatively durable to offer as "bait" to the attacker. This "bait" part of your anatomy is usually a leg or arm, parts which can withstand considerable forces without serious injury to yourself; even if bone breakage occurs from this offered "bait" part of your anatomy, you can make a successful defense which would not be the case if the chain connected with a more vital area of your anatomy.

The meatcleaver is a particularly difficult weapon to defend against, like the hatchet or any chopping device, because of its weight and the momentum it generates as it chops at you. Special tactics must be used to ensure protection.

Facing a razor-wielding assailant has a blood-chilling psychological effect against all but the most experienced defender. Like encounters with other sharp or bladed weapons, it is difficult to come out with no injury to yourself. Limited to slashing or hacking tactics, the razor cuts cleanly and deeply with an ease ordinary blades lack. If you offer some " target " as bait while you protect more vital areas, be sure that the target area is adequately padded. If this is impossible, you have no choice but to face the consequences. Consecutive "baits" may be offered, and if such is the case, the alternation should be made from extreme separations of distance between them, that is, a hand held high as one "bait", followed by a foot, held low, etc., is best. Offering the hand, continually at one level, permits the attacker to get set for a possibly fatal attack.

No attack action is recommended against a razor-bearing assailant. All responses in this Chapter are defensive responses provoked by an attacker giving the defender no choice but to move in defense of himself. Here again you can either get *inside* the swing radius, or keep *outside* of it. Staying outside is purely defensive and is the best policy for the average man, who should look for the best chance to escape by running. Getting inside the swing radius calls for a sureness of continued action that will keep the razor from cutting.

Often your surroundings will force you into one pattern or the other, but if you can choose, keep *outside* the razor swing. Regardless of what you do, do it with the attitude that perhaps your first response *will not* satisfy the situation. Keep a constant vigilance that will enable you to continue your defense. Bear in mind that a razor wielding attacker need not be treated with conservative kindness. He is after your life!

All responses described in this chapter must be practiced with a training partner(s). Begin slowly, so that you come to understand just what you must do. Gradually build up speed, both with the attacks and your responses. Seek to build automatic reactions to the situations by practicing several times per week.

Practice in normal daily dress and do not limit yourself to the luxury of the smooth, flat surface of a gym floor. Get out on grass, gravel, and unpaved surfaces in order that you may savor some of the realities of these situations as they might happen. The responses are given in terms of one side, right or left, but in many instances, by simply using corresponding instructions you can make the response work on the other side.

FRONTAL FREE THREAT-SWITCHBLADE

Situation: A frontal assailant, holding a switchblade knife in his right hand, is threatening you, but has not yet opened the knife. You have plenty of room in which to maneuver.

95

Response: Stand in the left front-facing posture. You must be prepared to go into action as the assailant opens the knife. Deliver a fast and accurate front snap kick (slightly roundhouse), directly into his knife hand (right), aiming for a point on his inner wrist. Pictures above and below.

Immediately after making kicking contact, step the kicking foot to the ground to a position between his feet. Diagram, next page. As your foot settles onto the ground, place a hard Knife-hand Block against his knife hand at a point near his wrist. Top pictures, next page. Grasp his right arm with your right hand after the blocking action

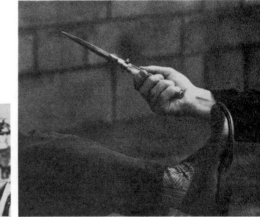

and pull his right arm forward and downward as you twist fast to your right, keeping both feet in place. Deliver a left Fore-fist over the top of his right arm, hard into his right side head or facial region, timing the blow with the twist of your body to the right. Bottom picture. The final action can be seen on the next page.

Keypoints: The peculiar weakness of the average switchblade knife lies in its inability to be opened while grasping it firmly in one hand. Your attack must take advantage of this; as the knife clicks open, your kick must arrive at the target or the situation will deteriorate to that involving an ordinary knife. Kick to knock the knife out of the assailant's hand. If you miss the kick timing or the target, you can deliver a Foot Edge or rear kick from the position shown in the top right pictures on the preceding page.

FRONTAL FREE THREAT-CHAIN

Situation: An assailant has you backed up against a wall; you are cornered. He is swinging a chain with his right hand, threatening to beat you with it. You have very little room to move.

Response: Meet the assailant in a right front-facing posture, offering your right leg as "bait". As he swings the chain at your face, rock backward, keeping your feet in place, to avoid the chain. Top picture. On the backward stroke he manages to ensnare your baited advanced right leg. Middle and bottom pictures.

The assailant begins to haul you in with the chain wrapped around

your right leg. Go with the pull and turn your body so as if to back into him, placing both of your hands on the ground in front of you; support your weight on those hands and on your left leg, knee well-bent and well under you. Pictures. Allow yourself to be pulled/dragged closer to the assailant, but keep enough resistance to keep yourself from being overpowered.

When your assailant slacks off on his pull, place your ensnared foot firmly on the ground and support yourself on your hands and this foot; lift your left foot from the ground and bend your knee. Top picture. Immediately drive a back kick hard into the assailant's knee, groin, or mid-section (shown), using your left heel in a thrusting motion. Middle and bottom picture.

He may drop the chain, but regardless, step your kicking left foot to a position forward and outside of his left foot (diagram left) and also step forward with your right foot. Twist your hips fast to your right and turn a bit to face into him moving your right foot as shown in the right diagram, and bottom pictures. Deliver a stinging Back Fist or Knife-hand into his facial region with your right hand; draw your left arm alongside your body, hand held as a tight fist, knuckles down. Final actions can be seen on the next page.

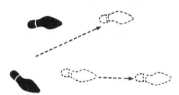

Keypoints: Do not thrust kick before he slacks off on the chain. After the kick, moving forward must be done with force and speed; if he follows you he will run right into your striking action, and you may not have to step back to meet him. However, if he stands still, you must step in on him.

FRONTAL FREE THREAT-MEATCLEAVER

Situation: A crazed assailant has trapped you and is intending to attack you with a meatcleaver. He faces you frontally. There is room to move, but the ground is uneven.

Response: At his attack, he grabs your throat or lapel with his left hand; do not let this distract you. He brandishes the meatcleaver overhead preparatory to chopping it downward onto your head. With the downward stroke of the meatcleaver arm, drive an X-Block, either hand on top (right shown), hands held as tight fists, hard up under this attacking right arm; contact it just above his wrist from underneath. Pictures.

Immediately after the blocking action, grasp his attacking arm with your right hand and pull that arm forward and downward as you twist forcefully to your right; accelerate the pulling force by simultaneously stepping a bit backward with your right foot and pivoting your left support foot to the right. Diagram, and pictures across top.

Deliver a swift Front Knee kick (slightly roundhouse), using your rearmost right leg, hard into his groin region as you twist fast to your left; continue your downward and forward pull on his right arm. Bottom picture. The final action may be seen on the next page.

Keypoints: The block-grasp-pull must be a continuous action, timed with your backward step and twist of your body to the right. The second twist, to your left must be timed with the kneeing action; your left hand may detach to be placed as shown.

108

FRONTAL FREE THREAT-RAZOR

Situation: You are faced by a frontal assailant with an opened straight razor held in his right hand at chest height; he has bound or taped the razor in an open position. He stalks you. There is considerable space in which to move, but the ground is uneven.

Response: Stand opposite to his stance (right shown) by taking a left front-facing posture; keep your hands at belt height close to your body in front of you, but do not form fists tightly. He slashes downward diagonally across your body to his left; do not close in but rather anticipate a backhand upward slashing action by keeping alert. At the backhand swing, step backward to your right, toes pointing away from the assailant and bend that knee as you lunge over your right leg in the direction of your step. Keep looking at your assailant. Top pictures.

Having missed his backhand slash, the assailant raises the razor over his head preparatory to a downward roundhouse stroke. Turn quickly to directly face him and fake an attempt to block his upraised razor-bearing right arm with your left Knife-hand Block action; return to an erect position from the lunge to do this, sliding your rearmost right foot up a bit if necessary to keep your balance. Top pictures next page.

Your fake will make him speed up his downward roundhouse slash. Check any forward motion you may have and rock backward out of the swing radius of the descending razor, pivoting quickly backward around to your right by taking your right leg in an arc around behind you and twisting hard from your hips. Middle picture and diagram. Deliver a fast and hard Foot Edge or rear heel kick into the assailant's open right side rib area. Diagram and bottom picture. The final action can be seen on the next page.

Keypoints: Timing is critical. If you can jump in and actually execute the Knife-hand Block before the assailant slashes downward, do so, and deliver a fast front snap kick using the ball of your foot, hard into his groin region; it is better to continue the block into a single hand downward Grasping Block just prior to the kick. If your fake is to be effective, it must provoke him to a full, all-out roundhouse slash committment; a partial swing on his part may be dangerous to you. Your final kicking action must be done to the high target suggested, near and just above his albow; lower or higher areas will make your leg susceptible to backhand slashing. Get your leg out quickly after the kick and be alert to continue your defense.

Chapter Four
HANDGUN ATTACKS

ASSAILANTS armed with either a handgun, rifle, or shotgun, are extremely dangerous persons to cope with. They may be rank amateurs or professional killers and only if you are expert in firearm weaponry may you discover their talents. Working alone or in pairs or even in small groups, they commonly attack with the purpose of restraining their victims until their purpose and escape has been effected. Also possible is a direct threat to life for no other reason than personal revenge or psychopathic murder.

These weapons, used from frontal, rear, or side approaches to your position, can be employed from remote or proximate positions of the attacker. All of these tactics are very effective even against a highly trained *karate* expert. More often than not, assailants work in pairs or in groups with one armed member distracting the intended victim while one or more unarmed members of the group carry out the purpose of the attack.

Being attacked by one assailant armed with a handgun, rifle, or shotgun, requires a proper response by you if you hope to avoid serious injury or the taking of your life; being confronted by more than one such an armed assailant almost always rules out your chance of disarming them successfully. The complexity of the situations are obvious and compounded by environments, all of which make it necessary that you realize that you cannot afford to make even one mistake in these situations.

The responses in this chapter are developed for you, the average man, and cover only a minimum of situations. However, the representative examples will serve to show you that these responses are at best the most difficult of all defenses.

Practice with a partner(s). Begin with a slow-motion speed, working up to full speed "attacks" with the appropriate responses. Seek to build automatic response patterns by practice several times each week.

Use your normal daily clothes to practice in. Do not limit yourself to smooth, flat surfaces such as found in a gym, but get out on grass, gravel, or unpaved surfaces. Strive to bring reality into the situations for reality is most often not considerate when the actual assault takes place.

The responses in this chapter are given in terms of one side, right or left, but in both instances, the other side may be practiced if desired by simply applying corresponding instructions.

There is a tremendous amount of psychology involved when facing a weapon which shoots deadly missiles, such as bullets or shot pellets. Disarming the single gun-armed assailant is *only for the accomplished expert,* who in addition to physical technique is highly trained in the psychology involving disarming and who is thus able to react faster than the assailant can pull the trigger. For the average "victim" of armed attacks by handgun, rifle, or shotgun, the smartest advice to be heeded is "give the assailant what he wants", don't try to resist him or challenge him, and above all, don't try to disarm him. There are already enough dead would-be "heroes" and police widows.

When accosted by the ordinary gun-carrying thug who has turned the gun on you and is giving you commands about what he wants you to do, keep in mind that he does not mean to shoot you, or he would already have done so. He means primarily to restrain you at gun point, while he completes his mission, usually robbery. He is a coward, his use of the gun to back him up proves that, but the weapon makes him a "tough guy"; just remember, coward though he may be, it *does not* rule out the possibility that he may shoot you.

Most cases which involve a victim being shot under these circumstances, are the direct result of stupidity on the victim's part. Sudden panic, screaming, sudden movement, or an unexpertly made attempt to escape or disarm, can all easily backfire and cause the gunbearing assailant, coward though he is, to shoot you. Keep your head, listen carefully to him, and do exactly what he says. The amount of things or money he may steal, or the indignities or even indecencies imposed upon you or others, is a small price to pay for keeping your life and that of others involved, and is always far less than the value of a possible hospital bill, or your funeral fees, if you respond against his wishes and he shoots you. A better deal involves simply doing what he says. He gets what he wants and you keep your life—an even deal under the circumstances as far as he is concerned. Don't change the odds; don't be a "brave" guy.

This chapter, thus, does not recommend any of the techniques of disarming for the average citizen under ordinary circumstances involving an assailant with a gun. However, in defense of your life or those of others if you are convinced that you are facing a psychopathic killer, you have no choice but to attempt disarming and/or escape. In such cases, the assailant bearing a gun, is a killer; *he wants to kill you* and will shoot you almost without any reason. Proximity to the assailant is then *a must* and you must catch him off guard to be effective. This is more easily said than done, for each individual assailant follows no set pattern. It is also more easily said than done, for time may work against you and he may pull the trigger before you can go into action.

You may try to distract, stall, and lead the crazed killer into a direct off-guard position; usually this will have to be done with convincing words or feigning any condition which promotes your chances. Each case will be different and no general rules can be set to guarantee your safety. When you go into action, it is very similar to jumping from an airplane and using a parachute. There will be no second chance, *you must do it right the first time!*

FRONTAL FREE THREAT

Situation: Your assailant, holding an automatic pistol in his right hand, has ordered you to raise your hands. He is out of range of your hands. You are standing on uneven ground but you have a lot of space to move around in.

Response 1: The assailant is definitely distracted. Timed with his distraction, deliver a swift and accurate front snap kick, using the ball of your right foot, hard into his gun hand from underneath, using sufficient force to knock the gun from his hand. Pictures top and bottom.

Quickly step that kicking foot to the ground directly in front of him and deliver your right Forefist hard into his mid-section or groin, twisting your hips hard to your left as you punch. Keep your feet in

place during this action, and bring your left arm along the left side of your body, hand formed in a tight fist, knuckles downward. Top pictures. Rapidly punch your left Forefist into his groin or mid-section (shown) by twisting to your right as you deliver the punch; withdraw your right arm to a position alongside of your body, hand held in a tight fist, knuckles downward. Keep your feet in place during this punching. Top pictures. The final actions can be seen on the next page.

Keypoints: Timing is vital and your response must only be attempted when you are sure of his distraction; to do otherwise may prove to be fatal to you. If he is not distracted, do not move.

Response 2: Your assailant is not distracted and has moved in close to you, poking the pistol into your chest as he threatens you. When the pistol is within range of your hands you may go into action. Do so by twisting fast to your left, without moving your feet, and bring your right hand, formed as a Palm-heel Block, hard downward and laterally against the inside of his gun wrist-forearm. Pictures.

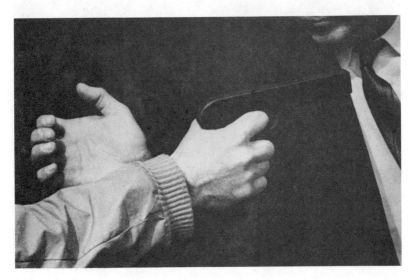

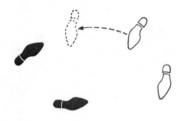

This blocking action must knock the gun muzzle out of the line of fire which would collide with your body. Drop your hips a bit as you block. Pictures previous page. Continue your blocking keeping, action contact as you quickly bring your left from inside of his gun arm, to grasp his gun hand, thumb pointing downward. Pull outward against his gun arm. Step forward and directly in front of his left foot with your right foot, turning your toes inward (diagram) as you simultaneously deliver your Elbow Forward Strike using your right arm, hard into his mid-section or groin. Picture above. The final action can be seen on the next page.

Keypoints: The initial block must be made with the feet in place; there is no time to move your feet. Hip twist and block must be timed together, just as are the left hand grasp of the assailant's gun arm, pull, step, and elbow strike. Tear the gun from his grasp.

FRONTAL SEARCH

Situation: A frontal assailant holds an automatic pistol in his right hand, close to his right hip. He is alert and has approached you closely enough to search you with his left hand. You are standing on uneven ground but there is plenty of room to move around in.

Response: Step your right foot backwards and execute a fast and accurately-placed Pressing Block with your left Palm-heel, hard against his gun hand from the outside; twist your hips to the right as you do this, drawing your right arm alongside of your body, hand held as a tight fist, knuckles downward. Pictures this page.

Drive a fast Forefist, using your right hand, hard into the assailant's facial area as you continue pressing Block action against his gun hand; do not move your feet as you deliver this punch, but twist hard to your left with the punch. Pictures, next page. The final action can be seen on page 128.

Keypoints: Your block must place the line of fire out of collision course with your body. Continuous pressing action is necessary until the fist strike is made; after this, it is advisable to tear the gun from his hand.

Situation: You have been taken from the rear by an assailant who is unmistakenly jamming a hand gun into your back under threat of shooting you. The gun presses about mid-back. You are on uneven ground and there is plenty of room to move.

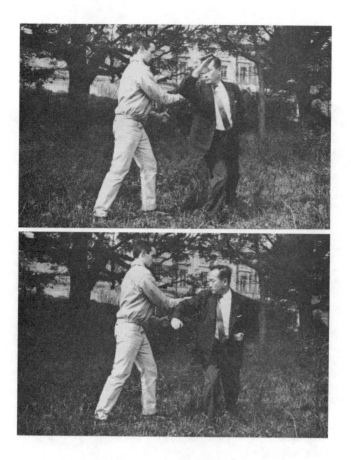

Response: Keep your feet in place but pivot as you turn fast to your right, chopping your right arm, hand formed as a Knife-hand, down and inward hard against his gun arm; contact his arm elbow to elbow. Drop your hips with this turning action. This action must bring your body out of the line of fire of the handgun. Top pictures.

Immediately after this blocking action, quickly smash your right Knife-hand Block against the wrist of the assailant's gun arm, grasping it and pulling him forward to his left front. Simultaneously step your

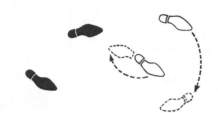

left leg around in a short arc to your left front, pivoting on your weighted right foot, to face into your assailant and bring your left arm alongside of your body, hand formed as a tight fist, knuckles downward. Diagram and picture. Deliver an Elbow Forward Strike, using your left arm, hard into the assailant's exposed right rib area by twisting hard to your right with the striking action of your elbow. Keep your feet in place as you twist and strike. The final action can be seen on the next page.

Keypoints: Your initial blocking action must be elbow to elbow contact; your Knife-hand block is made after such contact. Continuous action with the grasp, pull, step, and strike after the initial block, is essential for your safety. Tear the gun from his grasp.

132